# Anubhav

## (An experience of our lives)

Pranshu

**Title - Anubhav : An Experience of Our Lives**

| | | |
|---|---|---|
| **Author** | : | Siddhant Sharma and Avinash Singh Thakur |
| **Publisher** | : | Siddhant Sharma"Pranshu"<br>S/O Arun Kumar Sharma, Shiv Vihar Colony, Dhuma Road, Ganesh Nagar, Bilaspur (m.Corp), Bilaspur, Chhattisgarh<br>Pin No. - 495001 |

| **Edition** | : | First (2024) |
| **Printer** | : | S and S Publishers and Distributors, R. K. Nagar, Bilaspur, Chhattisgarh; Pin No. – 495006. |
| **Price** | : | Rs.380/- |
| **ISBN** | : | 978-93-341-6005-5 |
| **Language** | : | English |

# Acknowledgements

I extend my deepest gratitude to the following individuals whose unwavering support and guidance have been instrumental in shaping this poetry collection.

To my parents, Arun Kumar Sharma and Barkha Sharma, I offer heartfelt thanks for being beacons of inspiration and encouragement. Your selfless sacrifices, patience, and unwavering trust has made me the person I have become today. Your teachings and ability to focus on trivial details has nurtured my writing skills, providing a foundation upon which I plan to flourish on this journey.

My brother Sandesh, I appreciate your candid critiques and insightful feedback, which have refined my craft and pushed me to explore new depths in my poetry. Your presence in my life is a treasured gift.

To my cousin Vaibhav, I express sincere gratitude for entrusting me with this project. For threatening me of cutting all ties, if I don't write the book. Your faith in my abilities has been a constant source of motivation, driving me to create something worthy of your trust.

To Avinash Singh Thakur, my editor, I am grateful for your meticulous attention to detail, expert guidance, and thoughtful suggestions. Your dedication to refining my work has enhanced its quality and clarity.

To Himalay, Akhilesh and to all those friends and family, who kept on nagging me for publishing this book. I appreciate your love for my poems.

To Shreya, my muse, I am eternally and most grateful to you for igniting a spark within me. Your presence has awakened a world of emotions, thoughts, and experiences that have found expression in these poems. You are the heartbeat of this collection.

To each of you, I offer heartfelt thanks for being pillars of strength, inspiration, and growth. Your love, support, and encouragement have made this collection possible. I am honored to share it with the world.

Sincerely,
**Pranshu.**

‘hell_s_lost_property’

‘pranshu_pens’

***“I am, a phoenix,***
***Risen from the ashes and flames.***
***Flying off to the heavenly skies,***
***I may be a Heaven's reclaim, yet,***
***I wonder if I am Hell's lost property.”***

*Morning's hope is like sunrise, bright and warm,*
*With the setting of sun, becomes evening's wisdom,*
*filled with remorse each night you reach your bed,*
*You hope for a better tomorrow, new experiences ahead.*

- **Dr. Avinash Singh Thakur.**

# Anubhav

***Anubhav***, the Hindi word for '**Experience**', is a tapestry neatly woven from the threads of life's triumphs and tribulations. It is a journey of development, learning, and transformation and achievements where each step, every moment shapes us into who we are today.

Grandfather Pranshu, in this poetry book gives a tender tribute to the human experience, sharing his life's triumphs and struggles with his grandson Anubhav, and offering insights into the complexities of life.

In this book, Anubhav, the grandson experiences, childhood, the initial phase of Anubhav (experience), a canvas of wonder where curiosity and innocence paint our future. It is a time of exploration, discovery, learning and laying the foundation.

Similar to the Japanese art, Kintsugi, which repairs broken pottery with golden lacquer, highlighting the brokenness rather than disguising it, our experiences – both happy or dreadful – transforms us into stronger and wiser human beings.

As we navigate life's complexities, we search for meaning in moments, connection, and love. It is during this quest that we encounter our Muse, that special someone, unreal to eyes, or ears or skin, who brings exuberance, meaning and purpose to our existence.

However, life's fickleness can lead to heartbreak, shattering the glass house of our love and leaving us with shards of despair. We burn those pictures of our muse from our memories. It is in these junctures of gloominess that we discover our resilience. Just as the phoenix rises from ashes, we emerge from the flames, metamorphosed and reinvigorated. The experiences, though painful, become the golden lacquer that fills the cracks of our being.

***Anubhav*** teaches us, whether joyous or remorseful, our experiences are essential to our growth. Each second shapes us, strengthens us, and braces us for life's challenges. Challenges, not about avoiding pain but about embracing it as a transformative force. Our experiences bind our soul with our organs like strength, resilience, and wisdom, making us the masterpiece we are today.

***Anubhav – The experiences of our lives–*** is the essence of life. It is through embracing our difficulties and achievements, with all their complexities, that we rise from the ashes, into phoenix with strength, beauty, and wisdom.

## Stages of our lives -:

# Pursuit of Happiness

**Write your own little poem about your childhood:-**

"**Dear Anubhav,** as the innocence of a child faces the cruel realities of life, a child's pursuit of happiness becomes a strenuous journey. The path is accompanied by hindrances that test the very nature of their being.

Racism from kinsfolk, class differences among alleged friends, the loss of a parent, a single working parent and all the struggles eventually leading to the erosion of faith in a higher power makes hopelessness the child's home. In these darkest moments, the human soul unfolds its ability for persistence.

Family, the first haven of adoration and acceptance, for a child, when it reveals its ugly head of racism within the kinship, the sense of belonging is shattered. Deep scars from their heartless words make it challenging to find joy in a world that belittles one's very existence. Feelings of isolation and self-doubt seeps in.

As the child wanders into the outer world, outside the shadows of family, class differences among friends can cultivate aggravating feelings of inadequacy. The subtle, yet piercing, remarks about one's attire, appearance, facial features, neighborhood, or lifestyle can engender a sense of detachment. The pressure to abide by societal norms and expectations can become devastating, making the child question its own worth.

The loss of a parent, whether through death or abandonment, can leave an unfillable void. The absence can disrupt the child's sense of security and stability, in this unpredictable world. The single working parent, though an epitome of strength, may struggle to provide emotional support while shouldering the burden of financial responsibility.

The idea of a divine power can become more and more abstract. The question "Why me?" reverberates unabated. The loss of faith turns into despair, making a natural bliss seem like an unachievable dream.

The child, though dilapidated, discovers ways to adjust, to bear, and to endure the hardships that come its way. In this pursuit of happiness, the child absorbs crucial experiences. They understand that happiness is not a destination, but a journey; a dynamic process instead of a static phase. Child learns that absence of challenges can never lead the child to maturity.

The path they follow serves as a reminder that felicity is not a privilege reserved for the fortunate few, a rain that can be claimed by all, without consideration of events."

***"Through taunts, throes, and tears, thrown by thee,***
***I discovered the joy in being me.***

Pranshu

## Pursuit of Happiness

I descended to earth, to repay heaven's dues,
Found parental love despite my past life's sin,

From crawling as infants on earth, I started walking on shoes,
Navigated through life, while karma possessed a grin,

Since Ganga awaited, our inevitable rendezvous,
Yearning for my ashes— legacy to be poured in.

Parents showed pride in the colour of my skin,
***"Isn't white as milk"***, exclaimed all of my kin,

Maybe I stained their ideals of purity,
Nonetheless, all of them loved to drink tea,

Borrowing colour from wheat, I had become my own bread,
As darkness was deemed defective by whom I'd been bred.

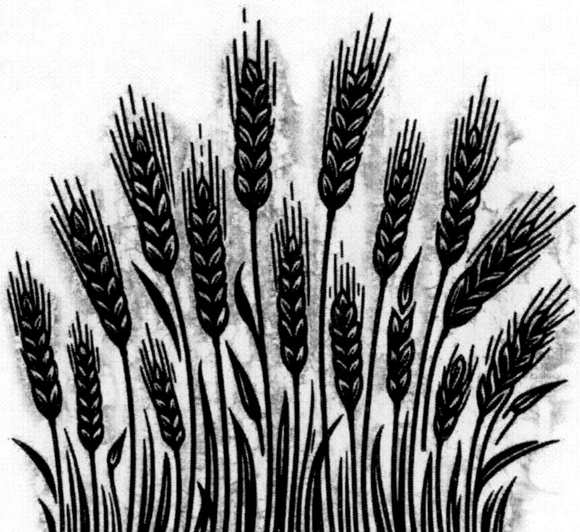

Pranshu

***"Papa, please, pick me up, put me on the seat,***
***Let us go for a little ride"***, I used to ask on repeat,

He told me often, ***"I have work son, in evening we'll go for treat"***
I used to sit near the main door, as he would come back with gift,

His bike's horn, a melody I could have recognized, from kilometers away,
My father, smiling at my mum, would always ask, ***"dinner outside today?"***

***"Hey Mommy, am I taller than you?"*** asked a kid in me,

***"Yes, you are,***
***My LITTLE son"***,
Replied my mom,

***"Thank You Mommy, my new chair is good"***.

Pursuit of Happiness

In a dark room, filled with hope,
Heart opened up trying to speak,
Watching him from a distance,
Was Brain calling him a freak,

The battle raged in a child's inner ring,
Heart's emotions against Brain's thinking,
Two foes clashed, in a struggle so grand,
Fought until death, to be the child's friend.

I was not hiding my fears
behind masks,
I would not have shed tears,
if nobody asked,

So,
what exactly,
Was I trying to prove?
Was speaking my heart that big a task?

Pranshu

Let life
complete
its cycle,
like earth,

And watched
wrath of sun,
giving space,
to the peace
of the moon.

I found a dragonfly,
A fragile life in my hand,
It withered,
in time's veil,

I stared,
at its colors fading,
thinking,
It is better,
to be dark than pale.

Pranshu

My heart was heavy, head wanted to get high,
I couldn't speak a sentence without a sigh,
For him to recover, I prayed closing my eyes,
Didn't know death has less chances than dice,

Time transfixed, I was stupefied,
I shouted, ***"Come out dad, where did you hide?"***,
Tears fell like rain, my body numbed in cold space,
Longing for his love, for his warm embrace,

Picture perfect family, scattered all around the floor,
Went to mom for solution as I couldn't take it anymore,
People had come, they tried to sympathize,
Yet I found comfort in the memories that still survives,

I remembered his smile and his laughter,
His guidance for the life, I had to live after,
Remembered the yearly trip we had planned in May,
And the way he hugged me every single day,

He was gone, the reality took time to sink in,
***'Does Yamraj take bribes?'***, was all I was thinking,
***"Life goes on, Dad ...and yes, I have moved on too,***
***Your son has become wise, after what he'd been through"***.

In secret, we lit the flames of equality,
I breathed matriarchy, passively smoked patriliny,
Her independence — a quite lesson for me,
As mom went to work, shattering norms of misogyny,

Ambitions sparked to become renowned and rich,
Even if I had learnt to cook in her absence,
I still yearned to earn two meals in this glitch,
Since feminism existed in home — in the right balance.

Pranshu

Should have never crossed
the black cat's path,

Bad luck,
followed me
back home.

Swept aside by Waves, on beaches I once knew,
Survived on fragile cowries, I barely owned,
Tattered clothes and worn-out frame and shoe,
Washed with water — needed to be loaned,

Simple lunches— nothing fried in oil,
I skipped school trips, told lies, ***"Grandma has died"***,
Teased, mocked and bullied for my toil,
In my home, powerless, helpless, alone I cried,

An outcast, a featherless cuckoo away from town,
While city hall was crowded with crows,
No night out invitations, no secret gifts, found,
Poverty made me invisible to the people I held close.

Pranshu

Pursuit of Happiness

Can't we be thoughtful once?
Are we that afraid?
Our thoughts are destroying us,
Happiness turning into dread,

Why cannot we stay silent?
Changing shapes like cloud,
But silence is a killer too,
Thunder awaits, thus loud,

Our world expands,
From tiny-tiny exhales,
Neither from undiscovered lands,
Nor from unspoken tales.

Tears dripped from my eyes,
Surrounded by salty water I was then,
I amassed so much inside,
Looked like I had become an island,

The tides of grief, they rise and fall,
Waves of loss, broke down my wall,
I held memories, to contain the pain,
But the weight of sorrows threatened to remain.

Pranshu

***"O' cloud, at you, I'll throw a stone,***
***If it hits, don't cry, don't you dare rain,***
***I seek not to disturb your peaceful sky,***
***But to aware you, life's storms pass by,***

***It happens to all, in this shared human plight,***
***We stumble, we rise, each day and night,***
***Your darkening colour, is weight that one bears,***
***Move on, society is like this, no one cares."***

Bought tickets
to a rollercoaster ride,
To enjoy
ups and downs,
for one last time.

Pranshu

# Pursuit of Happiness

Did they look at that smile on my face?
I looked happy,
At least I seemed so,
How did everyone like that?
I was an introvert with some social skills,
They did not notice.
Did they like my act?

To that childhood friend who had said,
***"Speak less, you do not want people,***
***to run away from you"***,
Was my knowledge unbearable for their brain cells,
Or I really talked crap,
For them to go ***"shuu shuu?"***,

Did I make them that uncomfortable?
Did they feel unsafe?
Or when I whispered in their ear,
Did I make them sweat?

I was a good person,
when it came to my heart,
It was not me,
Their prejudices were a threat,

Had they ever wanted
to really have a conversation with me?
As I spoke,
They asked, ***"Are you high?"***
When I just wanted
to get close to someone,
Was I wrong,
when, I was just trying
to make them smile?

It was not that,
I did not know
how to talk to elders,
I just chose wrong words then,

I knew,
I used to bottle up things inside,
burst sometimes,
yet,
did not mean anything
that I ended up telling them,

At times they had said,
***"Your words are powerful"***,
And I kept speaking to everyone
because of those few,
I smiled, looked happy,
How did they like that?
Was I good as an introvert?
Or
Did they like my new act?

Pranshu

I walked on wet footway,
balancing my joy and pain,
I found my footing,
one step at a time again,

Muddy puddles on both sides,
with fear of dirt on new shoes,
I walked with caution,
or my new character could be public news.

# Anubhav – The experience of our Lives

I discoursed about braids and bun sticks,
and had a fine receding hairline,
I could talk about the skin type,
with acne all over this body of mine,

Told people about beautifully coloured nails,
and had my own covered with dirt,
Asked about architecture and designs,
with a room of kid and passion of expert,

I spoke of fashion, with worn out shoes,
Discussed on traveling, from my balcony's views,

I could talk about stars and comets and planets,
and wouldn't even look once at the sky,
Conversed about plants and animals
with just pictures in my mobile,

Said things about festivals and customs,
and didn't know a single story behind them,
Told people about battles and wars,
Without knowing all its victors and harm,

Cooking was my passion, no matter taste or colour,
Conversations ignited, and that was all that mattered.

Talked about all the elements in Earth's crust,
hoping none of it was a part of chemistry,
I could discuss about someone's past,
Any way my favourite subject was history,

And maybe I could just talk about myself,
Because, I could talk about things I knew vividly,
I just believed in a good conversation,
It didn't necessarily need to be about me.

***"So, shouldn't we keep talking once in a while?***
***There is not much time in each of our lives."***

Pranshu

# Pursuit of Happiness

Tried different shirts,
To suit each occasion,
to blend seamlessly,
Ignored all the alerts,
gave myself reason,
To match society's tapestry,

Donned several masks,
Hid my feelings behind,
Bound by societal chains,
Performed all the tasks,
With only one thing in mind,
Indifference turns to acceptance,

Tried to shrink in clothes,
Built muscles for posture,
To fit into their frame,
Like flame for the moths,
Their brightened future,
Burnt me in this game,

Whitened tan-skin, dark circle,
Applied lotion and cream,
Lost myself in the process,
Must have learnt from people,
Despite being redeemed,
Society doesn't get impressed.

God created us uniquely,
each one apart,
Yet gifted us humanity,
to see equality in every heart.

(God has created us all
unequally,
And then gave us,
humanity,
to consider everyone equal.)

# Pursuit of Happiness

I broke the God more,
for each of my bone,
that false belief that I could believe him,
And colours he had shown,

Each failure was an attack on my faith,
which slowly tried succumbing my breath,

So,
all those theocrats,
Looked at this atheist,
I believed in art of the story makers,
And they believed in priest,

But turn back time again,
Who was I addressing?
Whom did I seek?
Was it the one I deranged?
Those were the voices I once trusted,
What had brought that change?

Was it the career path I could not walk towards?
or the girl who never became mine?
The family once I dreamt of,
or those dreams that never aligned?

# Kintsugi

**Write your own little poem related to your growth during Teenage Years:-**

"***Dear Anubhav,*** life can seem tough when we are young and sometimes it can feel like nothing is right in our life. Like the whole world is against us. But when we grow old, more hardships come our way. We become our parents' burden. We start feeling the urgency to make things better in our life. We gain the ability to improvise ourselves over time. Our imperfections and struggles prepare us for the imperfect and struggling world.

We can compare life with the ancient Japanese art Kintsugi, where one fixes broken pottery, here the pottery is us, with gold and silver lacquer, i.e. with friends, family and your emotional wellbeing. Instead of hiding the cracks, Kintsugi highlights the brokenness. Beautiful, isn't it?

***Anubhav,*** everyone's been there in initial stages of their lives - stuck in a furrow, complaining about their luck. We try to find escape in music. Music reminds us that we're not alone, and the world that listens to the same music is dealing with same adversities.

Whenever we are at our lowest point, some people might try to take benefits from us, pretending to be friends. ***Anubhav, learn to say 'No' whenever you feel like you don't want to help. Do not ever be a people pleaser.*** We learn to see through them later in our lives.

Finally, after facing defeat on each door we knock at, we reach out to something bigger than ourselves, like God, faith and spirituality. Slowly but surely, things get better for us. We find real friends who love us despite our flaws and faults, and we grow in their shadow.

We learn to work on ourselves, fix our own cracks. We gain confidence, and the idea of self-love inspires us. We start doing things we love, we travel, and meet new people, and among the people we meet, there is someone who's struggling like we used to. It's like we are looking at ourselves from the past. We realize, ***"Hey, I've been there too, and if only, I had not chosen to work on myself, I could still be there only."***

Just like Kintsugi, our scars become a part of our tale. We're defined by our might and weaknesses are lessons in our way. So, whenever life gets tough, always know this, our imperfections make us unique. Embrace them, and find beauty in the brokenness."

***"...And all those awkward smiles,<br>Will slowly fade away,<br>When those who didn't understand you,<br>Will start acknowledging your way"***

Pranshu

My fears of past
crawled
upon my face,
A relentless creature,
fed on my peace,

My whittled woes
writhed into wrinkles.

I sat there silently,
Looking at the paradise,
That was deriving the colours from my soul, and

The darkness in me,
When I closed my eyes,
Enveloped the sky, where my dreams unfolded.

Pranshu .

I robbed my bank account
in dead of night,
The police in me,
inept in investigation,
Found dust filled purse
growling in hunger,
After each heist,
as my belly burped in celebration.

To vibe on a song, I confronted past regrets,
In every beat, I found where I belonged,
With each take, I seized future's threads,

Dancing through life, I healed my wounds,
Each step toward knowing my wrongs instead,
I sought my presence in me or in sounds.

I wondered,
Why was the sky clear that day?
Was there a secret,
that clouds were keeping at bay?

No matter how much,
I gazed at the stars,
I was never going to reach them.

Looked at people,
Conspiring against me,
Trying to be nice all along,
I did not know,
What was making me skeptical?
Did not know if there was something wrong,

Why did I let myself believe?
In what happened to them,
I did not suffer in the same songs,
I sung the rhetoric of wisdom in my sabbatical,
If it bothered me,
I am happy I chose my own wrongs.

Pranshu

When I was asked to help others, I felt like being used,
Someone whispered one day, ***"you can say no to the abuse,***
***You can say no to anything you don't feel right about,***
***Just for once, try not to do things for the sake of clout"***,

I lost money, labour, respect, relevance for help,
Since I prioritized people pleasing more than myself,
I couldn't say no for help, on the cost of my own,
I aided everyone twice, thrice or more if it was someone known,

Exhausted my soul, to make myself feel more at home,
To stay in vision, of people I needed acceptance from,
Broke down the wall which I needed to protect my all,
Just made sure, I would be the first to reach, on someone's call.

With a shattered heart, I suffered a lot,
I looked for a moment to mend it again,
I had hoped that I'd get someone,
To whom I would share my pain,

But every time I talked to a person,
I realized I was better on my own,
The chaos I was in, about which cared none,
And how it was hard to let them be known,

Know what I was going through,
How bad I desired for truth,
As I cried in corner of my room,
With my mouth stuffed with cloth,

So,
I thought I'll work on myself,
Made a list of things I wanted to do,
Went on solo rides, read books from shelf,
Put on a smile and makeup to look beautiful,

I ate all by myself in a crowded restaurant,
Tried to make my soul strong once more,
Partied, danced, got drunk like a vagabond,
Walked alone to movies, stronger than before,

I attended public gathering for fun and laughter,
After long, I was able to tend to my soul,
Ready to challenge the world for what comes after,
I lost my warmth, as I started getting old.

Pranshu

I was a desert,
waiting for rain,

Being my own oasis,
I remained.

*"Dear God,*
*Once abandoned my dreams, I had found a new,*
*Mislead by thousand desires, I worked on what I had sewn,*
*I could suck out my own breath, you let me live for a while,*
*Could've mercilessly ended in death, but you had forgotten my trial,*

*Dear God,*
*I was finding each reason to appear in front of you,*
*My soul abided by my heart, and talked the truth,*
*To let myself live once again, in your guiding light,*
*I laid down all my gains, and bowed to your' might,*

*Dear God,*
*I was at the shore, but I was drowning, it didn't seem like fun,*
*Tried to hold on a bit more, waiting to become my own sun,*
*Stuck in that moment, I looked at ocean, its majesty and its wave,*
*I hated my ignorance, I planned on holding myself up to my grave,*

*So,*
*Dear God,*
*I was finding reasons to appear in front of you,*
*My soul abided by my heart, and spoke the truth,*
*to let myself learn and grow in your guiding light,*
*I laid down all my pride and bowed to your' might."*

Convinced I was to have found people such,
By dedicating a few words and little touch,

These kindred spirits, with warm smile,
Would always meet me, over a phone dial,

They were perfectly able to change my day,
Be it disastrous or however beautiful it may,

Peculiar as I, everyone had some struggle to narrate,
In their company, I was more confident, **I am till date,**

I wondered how long they were going to stay,
About migrating to another city or would they delay?

In each phase, I reasoned with a new nature,
Maybe they arrived like seasons in my picture,

After each interval, under a different guise,
In whose shadow, my own worth, I realized.

Met someone like myself,
Scared,
Weak,
Underconfident
And naive,

Both of us,
Walked parallel paths,
Him and I,

Both balanced our lives,
With a subtle smile,
One of us abided by society,
The other did hide,

I became part of inner circles,
Of friends,
A secant line,
He walked alone,
couldn't even become a tangent,
Failed to intertwine.

Pranshu

The flowers that withstand wind,
Bloom despite adversity,
I found a company of friends,
Of wisdom, courage and idiocy,

Chronicles of life embroidered,
With flowers on top of hills,
And shells from sandy beaches,
As sunshine equally wilts,
Revealed each of our stitches,

Moments of silence, shared after
Hearing one another's ordeals,
Followed by moments of laughter,
That just slowly heals,

Each evening, city drive,
Every lunch or dinner shared,
Is where life's beauty thrived,
Letting you know, someone cared,

Trips ended, nights went back to sleep,
Friendship stayed, for whom I used to weep,
In their presence, Heart felt at home,
***You'll value them, once they'll be gone.***

Lacked toys, so I played with hope,
Couldn't complete Max Payne missions in the laptop,
Didn't have resources, I felt excluded,
Friends mocking, echoed in my empty closet,

My game targets kept waiting for my Nerf gun,
Eyes bled before parents, before I shot someone,
Went to game parlours to play play station,
Never had money to have one in possession,

Might have earned plenty in future, what for,
Wouldn't be able to drive hot wheels anymore,
Since, I became too big to play a child's game,
For games waited one-fourth of my lifetime,

Life's new games broke childhood toys,
Dead were the dreams of playing with the boys.

Pranshu

When no motivation or passion stayed,
Time passed and harder it did get,
So, busy with my idle days, afraid,
I fitted my hand in empty pocket,

Desired to work, with no goal in sight,
No jobs to claim, no skills to pursue,
Motivation's sparked, that I lost in night,
A void within me, had nothing to do,

My mind wandered, I stayed at home,
Felt a sense of stagnation in my fight,
I survived on my parent's alms,
I had become cold, with no fire to ignite,

I wanted a chance to breathe, I felt choked,
Stress haunted my hair, more my soul,
I let rain wash away, as I got soaked,
Hoping, sunshine next morning would make me whole.

I sat alone to think,
There was once a time,
I was a kid,
who fancied rhyme,

Jingle reminded me of Christmas,
Mary was a girl with sheep,
Life was simple for all of us,
Friendship was easy to keep,

Johnny used to make me laugh,
***Makes me jealous nowadays***,
I remembered how I enjoyed my life,
And realized,
***I have changed in so many ways***,

I used to enjoy house chores,
Studying was a proud activity,
Used to be happy home alone,
***I am now bored with everyone else in the city***,

Once fond of human decency,
Anime characters looked more alive,
Collection of coins seemed high profile,
Games grew in me a will to survive,

TV always helped me to discover,
Something that I could not do alone,
Words like soliloquy, procrastination,
those days,
Were the only things I had known,

I used to sing songs like professional,
Performed those amateur dance moves,
created paintings which were exceptional,
Wanted to go back to the good old days,

Good old days of villages and small towns,
Where phones seemed less valuable,
Life had its own ups and downs,
Even then,
life was fun and seemed stable.

Pranshu

Stopped seeking solace
in the falling rain,

Since,
I was meant
to rise.

Looked distantly,
distantly at the clouds nine,
to whatever memories I had stored,
for whatever future could be mine,

Looked far away,
farther away than skies,
to measure value of honest man's work,
for dreaming all my highs,

Looked closer,
closer towards the shallow pond,
to penance of my sins,
without having to be stoned,

Looked at myself,
Myself and my own reflection,
As my sad face became a grin,
As I let rain pass for a new sun.

Pranshu

Sent my dreams
on an outing,

So,
I could work on them,
after
they had
seen
the world.

Worked out,
When I had gotten time,
For future,
Did not save my grief,

Stepped up the loads,
even in moments of disbelief.

Pranshu

Kept my head low,
Tried to look at myself more,
I needed to form iron now,
By working on this ore.

With each strike, my value would've grown,
Through the flames I would've risen anew,
Before anyone of them would've known,
I would've become stronger, wiser, in a different hue.

"I stood in front of you,
Without even saying a word,
Tried to act normal,
While looking totally absurd,

Had a cloth for a sunny day,
Umbrella for the rain,
I frowned and I smiled,
But I was ready to go out again,

Yes, I was very happy,
And I might've sounded insane,
It's just something I felt with you,
Which I could not explain,

So, mirror on the wall,
How could you even understand?
That when I said ***'Perfect',***
You are what I meant."

Pranshu

# Letter to my Muse

**Write your own little poem filled with feelings for your love :-**

Letter to my Muse

*"Anubhav, would you mind letting your grandma read this section?"*

*"My love, my muse, there were moments I wanted to assure, and reassure you, about your value in my life, but I couldn't find words fit to describe them. If only I could, I would have repeated the same actions to have you in my life again.*

*When you first appeared in front of my eyes, I knew that you were someone phenomenal, ornamented with both, beauty and brains. You illuminated my dark and gray world, as you filled colours in it, with each step you took toward me. I felt an inexplicable connection to you. Maybe I had met you in previous lives, and promised to meet you again.*

*You were unlike anyone I had ever met. You shone like diamond, with a contagious smile, and your' not-so-hidden quirks, all captivated me. I was drawn to your honesty, authenticity, peculiarity, and individuality. You were a breath of fresh air, a breeze of warmth, which transformed me in ways, I had only experienced in movies.*

*Being with you made me complete. You discovered the best in me, encouraged me to grow, to learn, and to explore. Your admiration and acceptance towards me presented me with the courage to confront my flaws and to commit myself for self-improvement. I have been grateful to you forever.*

*You were a dream come true. Yet, I felt inadequate, undeserving of your love and affection. But you found comfort in my presence. You confided in me, shared your deepest regrets and happiness. I cherished deeply, your trust in me.*

*Your "stupid little acts," as I called them, found a home in me. I adored your cheerful nature, your silly jokes, and your infectious laughter. You were unapologetically yourself, and I reveled in that liberty.*

*In your presence, I found solace. I could be me, imperfect and vulnerable. You saw me beyond my flaws, and appreciated my characteristics. I became the best version of myself, when I looked at you being my mirror.*

*"You were the melody that I sung, Your body a piano,*
*Each part a key, As I played the notes,*
*Your forehead sounded like kisses, Eyes fluttered like Polaroids,*
*Your fingers moved like water, Lips were confessions in your voice."*

*You have been my safe haven, my partner, and my best friend."*

As I walked past a place,
I watched the sky,
change its colours,
from a dreadful gray
to a brighter red,
never more than your lips,
and amid all those changes,
the voice of nature,
waited for your response,
as they fell in love with you,
your fragrance too,
I peeked from underneath,
Then I removed my hood to see,

What had made everyone mad?
Was it the almighty's grace?
But,
My love,
It smelled like you.

Pranshu

Letter to my Muse

There were oddities,
to describe
which,
I could not find words,
You
were one of them.

An oddity, I wondered,
was a work of art,
A masterpiece,
that transcended my heart.

You
will never,
get a
Nobel Prize
for peace,

You created
havoc
in my heart.

Pranshu

If my parents' love made me a poem,
You were the missing verse in me,

To be rhymed with my name,
To be recited beautifully,

In this poetic stage of world,
a poem one memorizes in seconds.

***"Would you like coffee?"***
I asked,

**"I will
take a sip
from your
lips."**

What gardener,
mate its beauty
with rose,

With garden
full of flowers,
You are the one
he chose.

I always
looked
into your eyes,

Somehow
you knew,
I wanted
those
lips.

Pranshu

When
I tucked
your hair
behind your ear,

My heart skipped a beat every time.
(Did your heart race?)

I would sit there
with a
slouched back,

Smiling
at
your
stupid little act.

Letter to my Muse

There was magic in the forest,
When you were near,
Fluttering of your wings,
music to my ear,

To my longing eyes,
Your beauty a feast,
The wisdom of a fairy,
Was meant for a beast.

How did I know,
The fairy was the one?
I watched this beast,
transform into human.

May be
I was waiting
more for
this,

for someone
to bring up
this
Metamorphosis.

Pranshu

Letter to my Muse

Why
did I look
in the night sky?
like,
I would see
an angel soon,

It felt like,
I
was discussing,
about you
with the moon.

Each day I told her,

***"Let me call you
every night,***

***While my heartbeats
be your
lullaby."***

(CALL +91-9893xxxxxx)

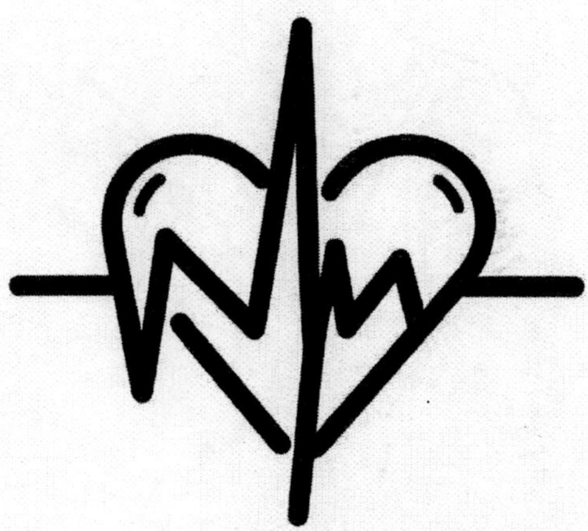

I had not,
in so many years,
Tried exploring the new,
I wanted to experience,
all the fiction I had read,
All with you.

Like a river,
I ran along the edges of land,
Every time I became
a waterfall instead,

I tried, yet lost,
my calm and composure,
The moment I reached you,
And came closer,

I smiled at you,
As sun shined bright over our head,
I saw colours in my life,
going from violet to red,

I sought the dark clouds,
And the gloomy rain,
So that, I could be filled with water,
And fall on you again.

Pranshu

Letter to my Muse

Our conversations would become a magical duel of wits,
You taught me lessons in which I resisted,
like Harry,

You as Professor Snape tried penetrating my mind,
wanting me to find,
my strength in me.

Being as fierce as Hades,
Speaking the tongue of a demon,

I wondered,
if I still liked hell,
While I was lost for a human.

Letter to my Muse

For once, I wanted to get caught,
For once, my phone to be checked,
Only once, to risk my privacy,
And my simplicity to be wrecked,

An intellectual policeman at first,
I wanted, with knowledge of love and art,
So, he could find out all the poems in my phone,
Which would have slowly succumbed his heart,

Poems, written all for you,
World would have known the crime I had committed,
Once they would have known about my love,
For you, they must have questioned God,
***"How did you create a beauty like it?"***

You told me, ***"you are air and water to my soul,***
***It's hard to survive without your role."***

I asked, with a chuckle and grin,
***"What about food? My dear Jelly Bean."***

***"You are the sun,***
***a shining star***
***in my life"***,
You exclaimed,

There were better ways
to mock
my baldness.

Searched the city streets,
Biggest of malls I had roamed,
Your love for clothes,
Had taken me to a cotton farm,

I had come back with fibers,
To sew myself in your life,
That you wear me with grace,
When the time would be ripe.

Pranshu

Letter to my Muse

I turned around every time,
to watch,
Walking in back,
what was mine,

With your little-little steps,
following me around,
my muse,
Your giggles echoed,
Your tiny hand fitted just fine,
Showering me with inspiration,
my rhythm and blues.

Tired of describing my life,
Everyone would have asked again,
So, when they would have done it next time
Could I have just taken your name?

That when they would have asked me to smile
As I would have worn a sad face,
Could I have spoken only of you?
And about our beautiful days,

That when hunger would have stricken my guts,
Would you have been my favourite food?
Could you have become my peace?
If I would have behaved a little rude,

That in a huge crowd,
Could I have searched for your face?
And if someone would have asked for my home,
Your name could have been my address.

Pranshu

Letter to my Muse

No matter the distance,
We had in between,
Displacement was always zero.
- A long-distance relationship.

Our love story,
Was either a poem,
Or a prose,
Poem that reminded us,
Of harmony of rhymes,
Of two individual words,
Or prose,
That was filled with details,
Precise but complete,

Was it a eulogy or a monologue?
Eulogy for each other's sacrifice,
The death of one's happiness,
Over another's,
Or monologue of one's internal voice,
Advising us to act otherwise,

Maybe it was a ballad,
To be sung by nightingales,
about our tales,

About the epithalamion,
Wouldn't that have been a beautiful ode?

It was a journey,
From a fiction to autobiography,
The fictional future we had realized together,
And the arrival of a harsh reality,

But everything seemed beautiful,
As we tried writing our romantic novel,
Which looked like drama,
To the rest of the world.

Pranshu

# Burnt Pictures

**Write your own little poem about your first heartbreak:-**

## Burnt Pictures

*"**My Muse, even though we had so much love between us, there were times we had conflicting emotions, due to my incompetency to make our love secure, with job and with stability. Maybe you taught me how I could become a better man, for my next love. Maybe for yourself.**"*

"Love stories are never just petals along the way. When we try to hold onto the embers of the initial phase of love, its thorns may bleed us. Breakups can be heart wrenching. When we lose someone we love, those embers burn us. We try to burn their pictures, throw away their gifts, and face suicidal thoughts every day. It is never easy.

At first, we blame our exes for everything that went wrong. We argue with ourselves, to conclude whose fault it actually was. We replay past arguments and dreadful moments in our heads. But as time passes, we start blaming ourselves, unable to find the courage to reach out to our exes again. We find ourselves in a vicious cycle of anger and pity.

Some people indulge in alcohol or substances to numb the pain. While others jump into different partners or hookups. But these coping mechanisms worsen the condition of the person.

In a very rare event, we run into our ex and reminisce about our old times. Its bittersweet memories, we hold onto, considering them our experiences. After a brief discussion, we understand we are better off apart.

Even if we think we have moved on, watching happy couples, when we sit at a cafe alone, brings back all the emotions. We remember what we lost, by not valuing what we had. Our mind wanders back to our ex, and we are forced to resist the resurfacing emotions.

It's insane how love impacts our soul. After a breakup, certain glimpses, sounds, or experiences can transport us back to the past, like our brain is wired to recall.

Reality is, recovering from a breakup takes an insurmountable amount of time. We need to be patient, kind, and honest to ourselves. We always have a soft corner for our ex, yet, comfort brings misery, and so do they."

***"You preserved the distance between us,<br>Every time I tried to exploit it with words."***

Society
Has
Never accepted
Lovers,

When
Sun and Moon
try to meet,

They call it
Eclipse.

(and get inside their homes).

Pranshu

You loved me deeply, heart and soul,
Despite my delays, without any goal,
But family pressure mounted, time ran fast,
Marriage awaited, I had yet to sail the mast,

I delayed vows, with unemployed care,
No family wealth, no future to share,
You couldn't wait, our age clocked by,
Longing for matrimony, tears ran dry,

Age's waves brought matrimony's shore,
I sailed the ocean late, still unsure,
Torn between affection and fears,
Our future hanged, between laughter and tears.

I was deaf,
even to hear
your voice,

and
I dreamt of mermaids.

Pranshu

We didn't know
about each-other,
We were so busy
in our tasks,

I asked,
***"Why didn't you tell me?"***,
You smirked,
***"You never ask"***.

We lived
in two distant worlds,
fighting
from our own,

You acted like
you were mature,
and I flaunted
that I had grown.

Pranshu

I was gazing
at
the stars,
only
to find the moon
missing,

I turned around
with tears,
to watch
her and cloud
kissing.

I wasn't the only one for you,
Maybe I was one of many of yours'

Perhaps I was just one among your many skies,
A fleeting light, in your celestial eyes,
You gazed at stars, while I shone bright as sun,
In those dark night, as I looked for my moon,

Our cosmic dance, had found its destination,
Your stars, could no longer make a constellation,
I had faded like dawn, as I shined brighter alone,
Leaving you with your stars, my dear moon.

Pranshu

You had
told me
so many truths,

I didn't know
which one
was
a lie.

Why did we stay silent when we were together?
It was contradictory of what we pretended to be in front of others,
Sometimes it was nice to see a different version of one another,
Sometimes we composed calmness, when we were together,

May it be a conversation on a daily basis call,
Or it could be us sitting in the same room facing our other halves,
Maybe we chose to stay so, as we had nothing to say,
Or it was possible that our eyes spoke, opposing tongue's way,

For a moment we would become deaf or dumb,
For a moment our senses could surely go numb,
We held our hands, filling the space or time,
We didn't use sign, even our words lacked rhyme,

Was it possible that we wanted to express something,
And we didn't possess words to justify our feelings?
Sometimes we waited for the other to open up their heart,
Sometimes staying silent could surely break us apart.

Pranshu

Burnt Pictures

In discussions, our emotions ran high,
Words cut deep, and tears denied the eye,
We longed to speak without fear of debate,
Not to explain, what we truly meant in that state,

Career, mine or yours', a delicate scale,
Paper love tore down in life's harsh hail,
**"Either us or our ideals",** a predicament,
A choice that weighed upon our commitment.

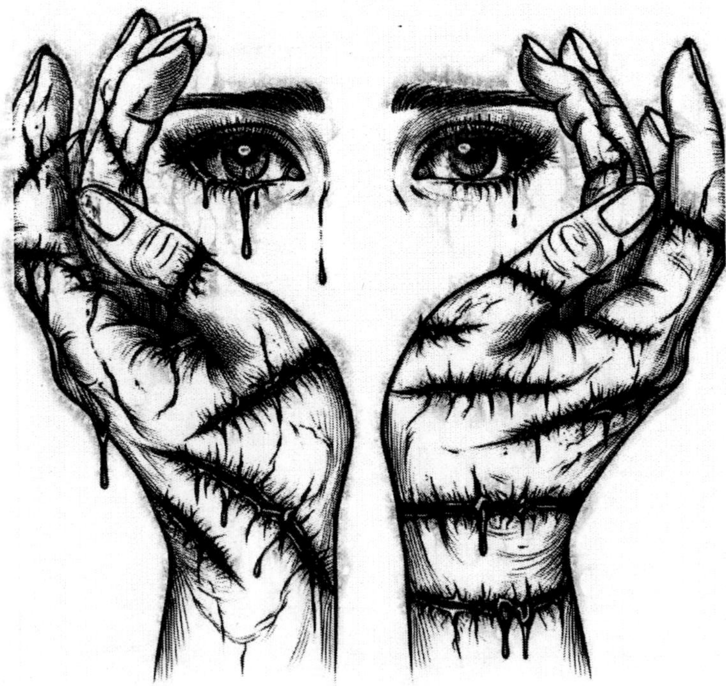

I didn't bother thee!!
Why did you even bother me?
One life was enough to see,
What you pretended to be,

To be my love, my friend,
To be the light in my low,
I didn't want this to end,
But I was better on my own.

(Anger takes control of our tongue sometimes)

Pranshu

I carried scars,
being wounded
by your words

I found
wisdom
in those lines.

I regretted
saying
those awful words
to you,

But
I could bear
regretting them,

Bearing you
still seemed
harder.

Pranshu

Feisty and fierce, I, a demon from hell,
Serene and pure, you, an angel from the blue,
You sought to present me comfort and light,
But I unleashed night, and it swallowed you.

The black cup you loved, a reflection of your soul,
Represented the darkness, that claimed our all,

The black coffee, which represented your heart,
A bitterness that consumed us, tore us apart,

Your darkness, once intriguing, then I saw despair,
Was the poison that infected, you and me, my dear,

I tried illuminating, each of your bitter sip,
Your black coffee consumed me, in endless sleep,

But I had to live, alone with a broken heart,
Reminder of our love, destroyed by your darkest part.

Pranshu

Burnt Pictures

In the washroom, I cried,
Muffling my voice,
I always blamed you once,
Blamed myself twice,

Where had I gone wrong?
I thought day and night,
Heard sad love song,
Repeated, Ed and Arijit,

Couldn't smile like I did with you,
Could get easily angry though,
Stuck to my room like glue,
Brain asked, ***"Out?"***, Heart said, ***"No"***,

Unkempt beard, and room dirty,
Punched walls, for physical pain,
Unlike you, walls couldn't hurt me,
I was afraid of falling in love again.

Why did you embrace hatred for me?
Did you not want my arms around you?
Could have passed your thoughts to my head,
I would've flown to vast skies,
If I knew,

Beyond hatred there was sunshine,
But it was bright no more,
I was neither yours' nor were you mine,
in this lore.

Pranshu

You asked,
***"When did we go into oblivion?***
***We did not drink water from Lethe,***
***I might not want to know anyone,***
***Still, remind me who you were to me"***,

I answered,
***"In silhouettes of forgetfulness,***
***You search for memories with me,***
***Though Lethe's waters you resist,***
***Your heart remembers what we used to be***".

It was the truth
we had decided upon,
That,
we were not each other's choice,

But they must have known,
when my head turned around,
Every time,
I heard your voice.

Pranshu

# Burnt Pictures

Went to the same place as before,
A couple's laughter, an eyesore,
Two cups, I ordered once again,
Aroma awakened bittersweet pain,

Laughter echoed, yet our love was silent,
Same taste, but it was somehow different,
Like our love, your chai got cold,
I drank mine swiftly, with memories to hold.

You left,
even before,
I could wave you ***"Hi"***,

Guess it is true,
Beauty fades with time.

(I THINK YOU SAW ME TOO)

Pranshu

# Burnt Pictures

One evening, I etched your name,
With my fingers on the clouds,
By time the sun had set upon the world,
Ink of your memories had turned the clouds dark,

In Twilight's hush, I heard your voice,
Like you, tender winds touched my face,
I cherished your fleeting glance,
And I knew it was a farewell.

After the soul left,
The desolate house, with faded paint,
Where joy was lost with time,

I changed bed sheets every night,
Sought fleeting warmth,
Love, a luxury, became a distant past,
Difficult to provide, even harder to last,

Anti-social activities I indulged in,
Started thinking I was Kabir Singh,

Abandoned shoes filled my rack,
Each day, with stories untold,
Blurred faces of nameless women,
Left at my doorstep,

In drunken haze, I searched for peace,
A stagnant rhythm,
Within drinks and lime, I drowned my pain,
A farce of pleasure, I had made,

Seldom, I heard my heart,
A light sobbing,
provoked me to walk,
on a different path,
A chance to heal,
to love my own self,
with zeal.

Pranshu

# Risen from Ashes and Flames

**Write your own little poem about how you imagine your future:-**

Risen From Ashes and Flames

***"My love, don't let Anubhav watch the last photo of burnt pictures, I don't want him to escape the pain of loss of love in drinks and multiple partners. Sit beside him, let Anubhav know the rest of the tale."***

***"My dear Anubhav, you don't need to experience each hardship or misfortune yourself, to gain experiences from them. You can learn from others' mistakes too."***

"Let us move on with this story. Everyone has been through brokenness and shattering of heart. But, let me tell you this, there is no better catalyst for growth and transformation than a good breakup. I know breakup is never good, but we have all seen the movie 'Shaadi mein Zaroor Aana'. Anyways my story is a living proof for you.

After a breakup, we hit rock bottom. Instead of wallowing ourselves in self-pity, we must find a safe haven in our support systems - our parents and friends. They pick up the pieces and guide us into healing.

Once we are through the process of acceptance of the loss, we must shift gears and focus on becoming a superior version of ourselves by throwing ourselves into studies and focusing on learning skills. Achieve our goals. Getting our love back can also become our goal. We must have one. Success definitely doesn't have a paved path. Yet, it has its own set of challenges. We lose our loved ones along the way due to differences or to death.

When we become successful, we must thank our family's wisdom that helped us along the journey. We must not forget to be humble, towards both strangers and familiar people. Never forget, we were there once, where they stand today.

Years later, when we return to our hometown and reunite with old friends, we should not just blabber about our success, but listen to their hardships too. Eventually, we'll end up discussing our old days. We will swap stories, laugh, and reminisce about old times. And in a crazy chain of events, we will reconnect with our ex. Trust the rein of time. We might eventually tie the knot with them.

My journey taught me very valuable lessons, which I am passing down to you grandson through this poetry book. I wish I could tell these things to my younger self. These verses have spoken of love, loss, and redemption. I may not have exactly planned a roadmap for you, but this will help you to navigate through life's ups and downs.

***"Heartbreak isn't the end, its flames cannot engulf us,<br>We shall rise again world hasn't seen a Phoenix in a long while"***

Bleeding heart, found bandages at home,
Warmth of mother's gentle touch, comforting,
Her belly's refuge became the memory foam,
In her wrinkled face, I found comfort for my hurting,

A teary conversation filled me back with strength,
In mum's company, heart started feeling at ease,

But with stories I couldn't share with her, I turned to friends,
After laughter and drinks, I drowned into her memories,

My heart slowly began to mend, again and
I vowed to chase the dream I'd put on hold,
As a new resolve within me started to ascend,
Heartbreak fueled my flame— forged me into gold,

Breakup's scars, though faded, propelled me forward,
As an experienced me tried becoming successful,

I transformed during each stage of life, altered
until Love found me, stronger, wiser, and whole.

I chose to leave my small hometown,
Had to seal some mouths on my return,
Didn't like the glass towers after taking a round,
Thus, something from life I did learn,

Mom's cooked food was better than a hotel,
I loved getting mocked by childhood friends,
Their voice echoed near my heart, I could tell,
But, longing to return could put my resolve to end,

I pressed on each day, every night,
To prove them wrong, who questioned me,
In those unfamiliar streets, I put up a fight,
To bring my muse back to my destiny,

Homesickness gripped, time and time again,
Yet I studied, to rise high, to make it through,
No one, but me and my dreams remained,
I had to visit my town, once I had risen anew.

Sometimes
I had to be
a lamb,

So,
I could be
the lion
I really was.

Every
smart person
is
a terrorist
of some sort,

Redefining,
justice and norms.

How much,
people love
someone's demise?

They await
a setting sun,
whilst
there is
a moon
at rise.

They negated my points without evidence,
I debated everything; I was avid hence,
What all of them deemed my nuisance,
Was awakening of a new sense,

Left alone, I worked for sole attitude,
A beacon of light discovered my solitude,
Never did I need to even conquer her,
As I always walked the path of conqueror,

Winds of doubt whispered, ***"Be low"***,
I stood firm, my roots grew deep below,
When I reached the mountain's summit
I loved how I told clouds, ***"...and so we meet"***.

Their roots were strong,
While I was a mere stem,
They stood above my crown,
As I looked toward them,

I faced the blows of wind
While they enjoyed the rain,
They had turned into fossils,
I became tree with fruits of pain.

(Now I have become a fossil,
It's a cycle)

Did bother, yet watched me rise,
They did not help me win,

I had come above them in heights,
Too distant to be seen,

They searched for me in the skies,
I didn't let clouds come in between,

So, when they opened their eyes,
They found themselves looking at me in vain.

Once,
I had shoes
smaller for my size,

I was ready
to walk on the world
bare feet then.

I saw the world with my sharingan,
People lived in my sculpted reality,
No one, capable of copying my feat,
I started impaling hearts like I was Kakashi.

Better hair, better clothes, better lifestyle,
Without even trying hard to fit in,
Met every other person with a smile,
Yet none came closer to my Rin.

There was a time,
When I was afraid constantly,
I know contrast was stark,
when my mouth was muffled with screams,

I know it wasn't my prime,
There was a part unrecognizable in me,
I might have looked like I was in dark,
But, my silhouette became bigger than their dreams.

Pranshu

Father told me once,
***"Never borrow money, put desires to rest,***
***A man with two meals, no debt, is the richest"***,

Mother taught me once,
***"Keep patience, it bears sweet fruit,***
***But wait longer, your fruits will rot"***,

Grandfather once advised me,
***"Always keep feet inside linens,***
***Earn and spend, not beyond means"***,

I learnt on my own,
***"Listen to your elders, to what they say,***
***They have lived life, that's coming your way"***,

There was a tussle,
between
my values and my knowledge,

Idea of selflove,
challenged
my upbringing.

I climbed too high,
to slip
back down,

Neither I owned
people,
nor the
crown.

Feet lied on the ground, amidst luxury's grasp,
Intentional choice, to be in reality's clasp.
Success's storms blew me off to the skies,
But I sought the ground, where humility lies.

On the ground, I had inscribed my name,
Trampled it before flying off to fame.
Yet, in lofty heights, I found what I lacked,
Wealth's cushion softened, yet broke my back.

Cold floor and insects, reminder of my past,
Retained ego's flames, from burning like moths at last.
Floor's hardness, all I could afford for rent,
In that vulnerable pose, I found my strength.

No pillow's comfort, replaced the peace of mother's lap,
No advice could restore father's views on mishap,
In an uncertain future, for the riches I had thought,
While choosing from antiques, rags were all I bought.

Pranshu

I left home to walk on skies,
Chased dreams, while lost some ties,
Faces faded like milestones on the journey,
Granny had asked,
***"Where's the saree you had promised me?"***

Highs exacted a price, brought me back to knees,
To cry, in front of gods to hear my pleas,
I farmed sugarcane when they lost their teeth,
Heard crack of their skull when I burnt my bequeath,

Memories lingered, of laughter shared,
Secret pocket money, by those who cared,
But time and ambition took them apart,
their part,
Settling emptiness, within my heart,

What was greatness for me? — I felt alone,
Like trophies in a house, without a home,
To know its hollow, the fame in the end,
I lost everyone while attaining where I stand.

I appeared happy, success had brought me friends,
with down casting eyes, were a little shy,

Like giant Mosquitoes looming over my head,
They wanted to suck my blood dry,

Their buzzing whispers fed on each of my thought,
Ravenous bites, diseased my life's goal,

They pretended to be, what they were not,
I swatted them away, yet they didn't abate at all.

Pranshu

After long,
Eagle found its nest's way,
Longing to meet
the Sparrows,
He had left in the village.

Donned our new suits, we had bought just the other day,
Casual tee and shorts could have framed us better way,
Shoes shined bright, not more than our faces,
Memories overflowed from our suitcases,

Scent of the cologne, I had worn—sparked an old lost love,
As I once was, she looked at me and then above,
Friends, were wiser, refined style, no more shying trend,
Behaved with elegance, with spouse and kids in hand,

Didn't jest thinning hair, everyone lost hair, wit, and strength,
Talked about ours past deeds, inside jokes— **still relevant**,
We visited those old trees, where we had learnt to fly,
Sparrows had become eagles, unafraid to touch the sky,

Talked about the town and people we knew best,
Left for a round, drove to streets where our memories rest,
Went to the same old tea shop, that filled extra sugar in care,
Drank a sip and remembered the time we all had spent there.

One day we get old,
Live in different worlds,
Travel in tailored suits,
From tees and shorts,

To walk down the same lane,
Avoiding all the dirt,
From well-tailored life indeed,
In tees and shorts.

Sometimes,
I looked at the clouds,
heavy,
looking for Pegasus,
to pass through them,
I even bothered
about Atlantis,
The non-existent
mermaid realm,
I sought the world,
and its creatures,
It was hard,
not to lose hope,
once none was found,
But,
I rode paper boats,
When
those paper planes drowned.

Pranshu

*"Planned to divulge my achievements and strife,*
*But alas, I could not tell my younger self,*
*To teach myself about the beauty of life,*
*That I wouldn't always be alone, God's there for help,*

*Now, I wish to pass on the wisdom to you grandson,*
*To be your mentor in life's variability now,*
*In your eyes, I find my own reflection,*
*These little experiences taught me a lot, Anubhav,*

*I have narrated my tale, of laughter, love and loss,*
*So, how did you fancy my memoir grandson?*
*I'll leave you, with wealth of knowledge and thoughts,*
*To relive my life under your moral bastion,*

*Make friends, try to hold on to them a little more,*
*Though unfulfilled, never be afraid to fall in love,*
*Respect your parents, they'll be the boat at your shore,*
*For rest, I'll be watching you from above,*

*You shall rewrite the stories better, where I had flawed,*
*Before you lose hope, give everything few more shots,*
*Wield wisdom as weapon to wage war against all odds,*
*When you get old, pass on to your son, these thoughts,*

*Address each of your struggles, tears and fears,*
*Leave a legacy, from your experiences through all your years."*

# About the Poet

Pranshu is a contemporary poet who serves you with his evocative and relatable works that explore the complexities of childhood, growing up, love, heartbreak, and self-discovery. Drawing inspiration from his personal experiences and surroundings, as he believes, one doesn't need to experience each adversity themselves to learn to live. Pranshu's poetry resonates with readers who have navigated similar emotional landscapes.

Pranshu, a wordsmith with a profound voice, weaves tales that echo the human experience. He has witnessed both the depths of plight and has yet to discover the exhilarating heights of triumph. His writing, a testament to his resilience, pours forth emotions like flower, its nectar for bees, that resonates with the downtrodden and the triumphant alike.

With each stroke of ink, Pranshu breathes life into moments, crafting narratives that mirror the complexities of the human condition. His poetry is infused with empathy and insight, offering solace, inspiration, and a reflection of our shared struggles and victories.

Through his work, Pranshu reminds us that even in darkness, there lies a glimmer of hope, and that every ascent is born from the ashes of adversity. His inspirations range from nature's subtleties to the nuances of human connection, reflecting his profound appreciation for life's beauty and complexity. He looks at everything in nature, to create your lives — a poem, using his verses.

This debut publication marks Pranshu's entry into the literary world, introducing readers to his thought-provoking and emotionally charged poetry.

***"I wrote poems about myself, afraid of copyright strikes,***
***Should not mess with God's intellectual property rights."***